PAINTING
THE
DRAGON

Anthony Jones

BBC Cymru Wales

AMGUEDDFEYDD AC ORIELAU CENEDLAETHOL CYMRU
NATIONAL MUSEUMS & GALLERIES OF WALES

First published in 2000 by the
National Museums & Galleries of Wales,
Cathays Park, Cardiff CF10 3NP

ISBN 0 7200 0483 7

British Cataloguing-in-publications Data
A catalogue record for this book is available from
the British Library.
Design and production by The Info Group, Cardiff
Printed in Wales by MWL Print Group Ltd

Cover: Local Passion, Kevin Sinnott

Rear Cover: Cyfarthfa Ironworks, Penry Williams

PAINTING THE DRAGON

Foreword

This book accompanies a BBC Wales TV series, broadcast in April & May 2000, and an exhibition in the National Museum & Gallery's Art in Wales Gallery. Both are expressions of the vigorous growth of interest in the visual culture of Wales, both historic and contemporary, which was a marked feature of the late 1990s. The Visual Culture Project at the University of Wales Centre for Advanced Welsh and Celtic Studies, and its publications have brought us a treasure-trove of images from the past. One of the great international auction houses finds it worth its while to hold annual Welsh art sales, and a London-based dealer advertises his stock of Welsh paintings on the World Wide Web. For the first time in a hundred years, the perceived impoverishment of Wales's historic visual culture, and its lack of a national centre for contemporary art, have become both a popular and a political issue. There have been calls for a Welsh National Gallery from members of the National Assembly for Wales and in the Welsh media. Many contemporary artists in Wales are also filled with a new millennial confidence.

At present the Art collections of the National Museums & Galleries of Wales must continue to share the Edwardian National Museum & Gallery in Cathays Park with the Life and Earth Sciences and with Archaeology and Numismatics. However our Department of Art is meeting the challenge of making its unparalleled collections of Welsh art accessible to a growing and far better informed audience. Later this year all our oil paintings and sculpture will be on the NMGW website.

In 1998, the Pyke Thompson Gallery became the Art in Wales Gallery. This was designed as a visual arts laboratory, focussing on both the present and the past, displaying paintings, sculpture and new media, in a changing programme of exhibitions. Several have explored modern and contemporary Welsh art from different points of engagement, for example 'Landmarks' (October-November 1998) or 'Creating an Art Community: 50 Years of the Welsh Group' (April-June 1999), others have surveyed the work of artists as varied as Henry Clarence Whaite (1828-1912), founding President of the Royal Cambrian Academy (January – March 1999) and the Cardiff-based sculptor Cecile Johnson Soliz (July – September 1999). Most of these projects have been collaborations, with our colleagues at the National Library of Wales, and with artists such as Iwan Bala, who curated *Certain Welsh Artists* (December 1999 – March 2000).

Painting the Dragon is also a collaboration, and the most ambitious to date. When I became Director, also in November 1998, BBC Wales was planning two series exploring the history of art in Wales from differing viewpoints, and had invited the National Museums & Galleries of Wales to mount accompanying exhibitions. Sadly it was already too late to prepare a show that could do justice to the first of these, the 'The Big Picture', seven brilliantly innovative programmes presented by Peter Lord in the autumn of 1999. The presenter of the second was to be Professor Tony Jones, President of the School of the Art Institute of Chicago, who writes movingly here of how the paintings in this museum inspired his long international career as an artist and educator. He also tells of how both the series and the exhibition evolved as a sort of 'home thoughts from abroad' and a passionate celebration of the art of Wales at the turn of the Millennium.

Many people contributed to the series and to this book, particularly the artists who were interviewed and who lent work. Tony Jones's own acknowledgements are on p.77 echo all of these. Focusing particularly on the exhibition, I would like to express my gratitude to those individuals and institutions who also generously lent to us, Lewis and Eileen Allen, Sylvia Crawshay, Edward Harley, Rachel Patterson, Cyfarthfa Castle Museum and Art Gallery, the Forbes Magazine Collection, the Glynn Vivian Art Gallery, the National Library of Wales, the Museum of Modern Art Wales, the National Museums & Galleries on Merseyside, the Royal Academy of Arts, and Wolverhampton City Art Gallery. I also thank Mark Evans, who worked on the project prior to his departuire to the Victoria and Albert Museum in December 1999, and to Oliver Fairclough and Arabella Smith who saw it through to completion. Loans were organized by Tim Egan and the exhibition was installed by Mike Jones and Keith Bowen.

Exhibitions such as this will continue to explore and celebrate the richness and diversity of Welsh art. They are, however, only one of the ways in which we will be contributing to a greater understanding and appreciation of the arts in Wales. Others include research and publication based on our unique collections. As I write, a two-year conservation survey of our 45 oil paintings by Richard Wilson is about to commence, funded by the Getty Grant Programme. We are also determined to present and interpret those collections, both in the National Museum & Gallery and beyond, to inspire in our users of something of the love of our visual heritage so eloquently expressed here by Tony Jones.

Anna Southall, Director,
National Museums & Galleries of Wales,
March 2000

PAINTING THE DRAGON

Introduction

In the last year of the last century BBC Wales broadcast a social history of Wales through the viewfinder of the art of Wales - images or Big Pictures which Peter Lord put into their cultural context and then interpreted for us. In the first year of this century BBC Wales complemented the series with a contemporary perspective on the making of art from Wales - Tony Jones garnered compelling formats and recurring themes from the studios of practising artists and then arrayed them before us with that millennium past and this millennium unfolding in mind.

I am immensely proud of both these brave Landmark series and of the teams of dedicated people who made them - led for the independent company, Element, by Richard Edwards and his Director for THE BIG PICTURE, Ceri Sherlock; and for BBC Wales' Arts and Music Department by Steve Freer and Chris Bruce, the Director of PAINTING THE DRAGON. The intention behind this ambitious two-pronged commission was, quite literally, to open the eyes of as wide a Welsh public as possible to the meaning of our visual history so that it might inform us of ourselves in the way we assume knowledge, maybe too readily, from the written word. These are different, perhaps ultimately more telling, marks. And then we wanted both series to do what every serious historical intervention must do by standing firmly on this spot at this time to cast a knowing Janus-look backwards and forwards. In Peter Lord, who came to Wales and stayed, and in Tony Jones, who left but ever returns we had series authors whose emblematic personalities were only matched by their expert witness.

BBC Wales - across all its services - intends to continue to put itself at the forefront of encouraging a deeper appreciation and broader understanding of all the arts in Wales. However, the visual medium of television is a wonderful electronic mirror in which to cast, in particular, for those images which painters have assembled and dis-assembled of ourselves, our landscape and our cultural signifiers. It is, now, too, that we can fully see that we have been, and are still, living through an intensely rewarding period of fine art practice in Wales. We need, in every sense, to supply public channels to let this endeavour irrigate the imagination of the new civic Wales that is inevitably emerging. So, let debate rage, by all and every means, over rooted traditions and global modernities, over social device and artistic purpose and over value and quality, but let it happen in a Wales where we can see the work continuously and permanently; in a Wales where related exhibitions and ancillary publications support on-going critiques and supply echoing insights for the next formulation; in a Wales where, leading from the front, the National Assembly ensures its own future home will not be merely one high profile repository of the decorative but the fulcrum, through a spectrum of public and private action, for the dissemination of Welsh art in and outside Wales, as the Assembly comprehends how vitally its own future public existence is caught up in the dreamy measure of an artist's private eye.

On BBC Wales television over the last twelve months we have had a full sense of how we are ultimately shaped and measured by that historical gaze as that essential series THE SLATE turned with sadness to celebrate and remember the life work of two great painters who died at the turn of the millennium - Ernie Zobole in 1999 and Josef Herman in 2000; two Europeans who, in different ways, found Wales' cultural experience and meditated on it in paint. And who can now doubt that we will eventually only see what the South Wales Valleys really means in our history when we finally meet Zobole's unflinching gaze? Or that Herman was no myth maker, only a painter of the Legend he encountered? Sometimes we need to be guided to see that painting the Dragon is not at all the same thing as gilding the Daffodil. And to that, more modest end, both BBC Wales series and this umbilical exhibition in the National Museum of Wales are dedicated.

Dai Smith
BBC Wales

PAINTING THE DRAGON

"Afternotes of the Presenter"

In 1999 BBC Wales and the National Museums & Galleries of Wales gave me a great treat, inviting me to come back to my native Wales from my home in Chicago, to present a four-part television series about artists in Wales, and to create an exhibition that directly related to the programmes. Both would be called *Painting the Dragon*. The artists on film, and in the exhibition, are only a personal choice but they are people and works that, for me, speak eloquently about how we saw Wales in the past, and how we see it now. I make no apology for my boundless enthusiasm in celebrating the visual arts in Wales, even with this small selection. As we concluded filming and making the final exhibition selection, the National Museum kindly asked me to write a personal note as a reflection or background to the whole television/exhibition venture. It's ended up being less a note and more a love letter.

I'd never seen an actual work of art, let alone a gallery or a museum, until I went to the National Museum of Wales when I was about 15. My family were from the far north, Mynydd Parys on Anglesey – I thought of Cardiff as the tropics … Eventually, transplanted to Troedyrhiw in the Merthyr valley, my obsession with drawing - and the influence of a fine painter and teacher, Colin Jones (1928-67) - led to my life as an artist, writer and arts administrator. I had looked at books on the art of the past, at prints of art works –yes, we had a print of Curnow Vosper's *Salem* ⌊ **23** ⌉ on the kitchen wall – but the shock of seeing an actual painting, on canvas, in a frame, on the wall of Wales' own National Museum, froze me on the spot. Art was not as ubiquitous or accessible as it is now. Art books were uncommon, and filled with rather dubious colour reproductions. Until that moment names like Monet, Turner and Cézanne were abstract and un-graspable, but suddenly I was confronted by the real-life experience of joining those names to the washes, lines, forms and blocks of colour that those artists had made. Revelation. Instantaneous conviction. I had to be one of them.

Bigger shock – some of these paintings were by artists who were from Wales, a nation I'd been led to believe had little visual art tradition. And that great art was made 'somewhere else', not here. But at the National Museum there were works by Richard Wilson, an artist from Wales who painted those gorgeous Welsh landscapes. Gwen and Augustus John were represented, the great Turner had come to paint in Wales, emigrants like Josef Herman had come from central Europe, John Piper and Graham Sutherland found inspiration here, and I saw the first fabulous works by Ceri Richards based on Dylan Thomas' poetry. It was a wonderful surprise, but bewildering, because apart from my art teacher in school, there appeared to be only one source of information, David Bell's book *The Artist in Wales*, published in 1957. And much as his fondness for Wales came through, he didn't seem very convinced about its art: 'At no time, since the Norman conquest, at any rate, has the Welshman had any visual artistic tradition.'[1]. Oh dear …

So the National Museum has always been part of my life. It was a teaching-aid for me as a developing young artist. Its 'Pictures for Schools' programme put real art on the walls of my school, Quaker's Yard Grammar School. As a result I saw George Chapman's dramatic etchings of the mining valley's landscape hanging in the corridors, and in my classroom I sat under the whirling mosaic slabs of paint that comprised Kyffin Williams' *Snow on Tanygrisau*. I went to the museum before taking evening life-study classes – 'drawin' naked wimmin' as my schoolmates called it - at the nearby Cardiff College of Art. I used it as an art history resource when I was a student at Newport College of Art. I even had my own sculpture exhibited in its galleries. And although my professional life in art education has been in the United States, Glasgow and London, I kept coming back to Wales, and to the National Museum, and watched as its collection changed and grew, seeing more contemporary expressions added to the old favourites.

[1] David Bell, *The Artist in Wales*, London, 1957, p.17

When the National Museum of Wales opened a new extension of its premises in Cathays Park, Steven Freer, television producer at BBC Wales, asked me to present a short piece on my reaction to the new galleries and their contents. I not only marvelled at the neutral light-filled rooms that displayed the art to its best advantage, but also at the art works themselves. Although it was surrounded and distracted by construction, the Department of Art had been quietly acquiring new works, conserving the existing collection, and planning for a major re-hang upon completion of the building. It was a collection that I thought I knew reasonably well. Wrong. It was a very different presentation of an expanded and deeper collection, filled with surprises, and names I didn't recognize. The story of art and artists who were from Wales, had moved to Wales, or were inspired by Wales, was told in a far more revealing way than I'd known, allowing for currents and connections to be seen that were previously hazy or hard to make. In that programme I noted that the position of the visual arts in Wales was changing, becoming more vibrant, and that the traditional cultural leadership offered by poetry and prose might assume a secondary role to painting and sculpture. That was in 1993.

This apparently sudden change in the visual arts in Wales surfaced again five years later in a conversation with Colin Ford, then Director of the National Museums & Galleries. Up to 1996 I'd served on the museum's Derek Williams Committee, where discussions about art and artists in and of Wales were a regular feature, and where a revision of collecting policy was being devised. Although I had moved, from the Rectorship of Royal College of Art in London, to the Art Institute of Chicago, Steven Freer proposed a series of television programmes, and the museum expressed interest in an exhibition connected to the broadcasts.

Although I'd not actually lived in Wales since I graduated from Newport in 1966, I was constantly in and out of the country. The National Museum had invited me to create a major exhibition in 1984 based on my endless research into the culture and architecture of Welsh Chapels, asked me to write the first book published on that subject, and in 1994 asked me to re-write and expand that text and re-published it. So the opportunity to 'come home' and reflect on television what had happened to the visual arts in Wales since I'd left, and work with the National Museum & Gallery on an exhibition was a wonderful opportunity. And it seemed to be an especially interesting moment, given the changing political climate. Art in Wales has always been about a pattern of immigration and emigration, about the flow of ideas entering and leaving the country. There's always been the power and spectacle of the landscape, and the industry that changed it, and many artists have worked on themes deriving from that change. But for centuries, many artists who were born in Wales have been enticed across the border in search of recognition and response to their work. However, what was appearing in exhibitions, books, catalogues, and on the pages of *Planet* was a distinct sense of rediscovery and revelation, of pride in the art and artists who were, in different ways, 'of Wales'.

When we begin to look at contemporary visual artists working in Wales, it's immediately evident that there's been a seismic change since the 1950s. There are more artists and more art. Some of it is being made by artists who are from Wales, some by artists who are not Welsh but have moved here. Some artists simply had strong Welsh connections, others came in and out of the country because their work is powered by ideas and forms that are rooted in Wales. Some have international reputations, and their work is to be found in major collections all over the world. In marked contrast to David Bell's comments in 1957, art in Wales is now seen as significant, contributory, studied, sought, and seemingly entering a Renaissance mode – perhaps the equivalent of the visual arts explosion I had witnessed in Glasgow in the 1980's. Art and artists of Wales have become of more central cultural significance within the nation itself, but are also part of the greater mainstream of art in Britain, and Europe. It's interesting to observe these changes while reflecting on a 1980s Arts Council report that said: 'We should regard Welsh art as a small but vigorous tributary to the mainstream of modern art … neither is Welsh subject matter as a whole adequate to sustain a separate category of art'.

Bell's comments are over 40 years old, and the Arts Council report was written over 15 years ago. Things have changed. Contemporary writers, artists and critics like Iwan Bala, Sheila Hourahane, Professor Tony Curtis and Peter Lord, have challenged and helped us to reassess the role of the visual artist in Wales. A new Centre for Visual Arts has opened in Cardiff, and the annual Eisteddfod exhibitions have become far more professional. Major new publications about art in Wales were revealing, in every sense of the word. Was there really a lot of art in Wales, but we'd not noticed, or has the notion of a national identity presented through artistic forms become a more viable (and valuable) intellectual and social currency, now that our own Assembly throws a light on the subject? As one artist asserted, 'Wales actually has a wonderful visual art tradition, but it became concealed - it just got hijacked by the more obviously visible poets, singers and actors.'

As we began to plan the exhibition and the television series we started to ask a number of questions. Why are there four distinguished histories of Wales, all published since 1985, that make absolutely no mention of the fact that Wales was both a breeding-ground of indigenous visual culture and a place of inspiration for artists who came to Wales, because it offered something that could not be found elsewhere? And what is that 'something'? How do we identify the 'Welshness' in the art that is made here – and some would ask if that actually matters? Can 'Welsh art' by made by non-Welsh? Does it really matter what Welsh ingredients go into this *cawl* of 'Welsh art' – is it a dish to set before the world, or is it only for local consumption? We were reminded of the pride Picasso felt in his roots, but also that the Catalans loaned him to the whole world. Was there a Welsh contemporary equivalent of Sir Nikolaus Pevsner's eternal hymn of praise to The *Englishness of English Art*? What will the National Assembly mean to artists – will it promote a Wales gallery at the Venice Biennale, Documenta, or the Chicago Art Fair? - I hope it's clever enough to do exactly that. What was art in Wales, and what is it now – and who is making it?

Is there any continuity in the art of Wales, a common denominator that joins the historic visual expression to that of today? Most would say that if there is one, then it's the landscape, the fundamental 'matter of Wales'. But what artists have made of that landscape and the things in it, are dramatically different. In a remote waterfall deep in the hills near Tongwynlais, you'd find a 4th century fertility ritual symbol scribed into the rock by the hand of an unknown artist. In an equally remote stream in the hills above Blaenau Ffestiniog, you'll with difficulty find a boulder carved from local wood, slowly moving downstream by the varying powers of water, made and put into that stream years ago by a known artist, David Nash. His work is a direct response to that Welsh landscape, as is the ancient work at Tongwynlais. But how does one connect across the centuries to get from one to the other?

What Nash, Richard Wilson, Ceri Richards, John Elwyn and Kyffin Williams make of the Welsh landscape is very different to what Ernest Zobole, Catrin Webster, George Chapman, Denys Short or Kevin Sinnott make of it. What a sculptor like Tony Stevens makes of the cubist forms of wet Welsh slate roofs in the Rhondda, is far from the sculptures of Welsh Heroes in Cardiff City Hall, or the Celtic Revival fantasies of Goscombe John. So what connects them? How does one tell the story of art and artists in Wales, and describe the thread that ties them together? It's a rich and vivid history, from the earliest Celtic carvings to the avant-garde technology of the cyber-Celt artists of today. And there's lots of it, a wealth of visual art across the whole of Wales, in galleries, museums, private collections, libraries, and in chapels and churches. The problem was how to try to tell this story within the time of four 30-minute television programmes, and the available space of the galleries at the National Museum & Gallery.

In the Autumn of 1999 a set of scripts for the television series, to be called *Painting the Dragon*, had evolved between Steven Freer and myself, and Christopher Bruce, who was appointed the director for the series. Chris brought a fine ability to rationalize the daunting mass of potential material into a visual form that supported the narrative, and knew what would make 'good television'. It quickly became evident that it was impractical to try to condense a 4000-year history into a chronological sequence. One of the main problems with such an approach was that all the contemporary artists would be crammed into the final programme, and it was the energy and work of these artists that I wanted to present. I wanted to know more about their work, and at the same time remind the viewer of some of the great visual themes and traditions. Even so, the list of living artists was so long that we had to make a short-list, and this was a painful exercise. I have very good friends in Wales who are terrific artists, and others who are Welsh but living in Paris and all across America – and they are not in the exhibition or the programmes. It hurt to have to savagely edit what we could put on screen or wall. If we'd had our way, there'd have been ten programmes and the exhibition would have taken over the whole museum.

We wanted the artists to reveal a broad range of expression, and be of different ages – so we filmed the most 'senior' artists, like Sir Kyffin Williams, the late Josef Herman and Will Roberts; mid-career artists like Shani Rhys James, Kevin Sinnott, Iwan Bala and Evelyn Williams; and a younger generation represented by Catrin Webster, David Garner, Angharad Jones and Michael Cousins. Even so, we were acutely aware that we could not include many artists who worked in complex installations, like Lois Williams. Some artists were abroad and not available for filming, like Bethan Huws and Geoff Olsen. We also had specific time constraints – I live in Chicago, but we wanted to film interviews in the studios of artists in Wales, so we had to timetable two shooting periods that would accommodate me, the BBC, the artists, and the access we needed in the National Museum & Gallery.

Simultaneously, we were working with the National Museum & Gallery on choosing the contents of the exhibition, with Mark Evans creating a long 'short-list' of works that might be included, and that we might have a hope of borrowing. This ranged from private collectors, the Lady Lever Art Gallery (for *Salem*, which they lent) and the Huntingdon in California for a magnificent Richard Wilson (which they couldn't lend). While we saw the exhibition as directly related to the television series, and the museum and the BBC coordinated the transmission and exhibition opening dates, not everything in the museum show would be in the programmes, and vice versa. The museum needed a long lead-time to arrange for the loans of works from sources other than their own collections. I deeply appreciate the patience of its staff to stick with this complicated project, even as it changed before our eyes.

Making a television series is a surprisingly organic process, and what sprouts from the original seed of an idea may grow to be a very different flower than the one you expected. *Painting the Dragon* was originally intended as a four-part chronological sequence, a pretty fast trot through many centuries of art. But as we discussed in greater detail how this would actually work, it seemed to us that, well, it wouldn't. So the whole series was re-cast, with the producer, director and presenter choosing, instead of a strict historic track, a thematic approach. The programmes would look at four themes that have been an enduring force for artists in and of Wales. *The Land* was obviously a dominant theme, as it always has been, and was the natural introduction to the series. The power of literature and legend, Celtic myth and the storytelling of The *Mabinogion*, formed the basis of the programme *Memory and Imagination*. The cataclysm of the industrial revolution and its aftermath was the theme of *From Heaven to Hell*. The final programme was about people, and how they appeared in the tapestry of art in Wales, which we called simply *The Figure*.

Once these thematic categories were established the museum reconfigured the list of objects for the exhibition schedule, to coincide with the programmes. A process of additions and subtractions began, always keeping in mind the limitations of wall and floor space available. Thus some large-scale works, like Clive King's huge and fabulous drawings that fuse Welsh Celtic images to Mexican Mayan and American Indian pictographs ended up being impossible, and the scale of all the works we chose is more intimate and modest. In order to make a coherent exhibition that showed the works well - gave them room to breathe – no more than forty works could be included. No installation art, no electronic works. But we worked hard to ensure that what we chose told a story – "maximum impact with maximum brevity" as Mark Evans said (given the wide range of periods and styles compared to the available space) - and were works of serious quality. It was not possible to show more than one work by any artist. We could not include any ancient art, no photography, printmaking, or much sculpture. And there are really interesting artists all over Wales in those and other media.

Wherever I was, in studios from Anglesey to Pembroke to Newport, I noted that artists would talk selflessly about the work of *other* artists, promoting their ideas, and wanting me to know about work of which they thought highly. The list of whom we'd like to have filmed and exhibited got longer, not shorter. I repeat, we only scratched the surface.

I asked every artist we met about a central issue – what's Welsh about art in Wales. You can imagine the range of replies, from its artists being important contributors to the 'master narrative of art', to its art being only 'painting in a minor key from a mongrel nation'. Art today embraces simultaneously a 'positive regionalism', and an overarching globalism in an international art market. Art made in and of Wales has to stand or fall in a world where art is increasingly commonplace and exhibited in vast quantities in galleries, museums, festivals, the art fairs and the big art biennales. If artists in Wales don't want that, and argue for an art that is so absolutely and exclusively of Wales that it ignores the world beyond the border, what does that actually produce? A kind of 'condoned parochialism', a kind of 'tolerable marginalisation'? I hope not. As a verbose but eloquent artist said to me "the real danger is the lowest common denominator, making Welsh-y Art for Welsh-y People, because then what you're saying is: It may be Poor Art, but at least it's Our Art". Tough words. It's a confrontational approach, and I thought of it in terms of the American regionalist painters like Thomas Hart Benton and Grant Wood, documenting the heartland, its plains and its people – very local, very specific. But there are always visitors, from every state and nation, clustered round Grant Wood's famous double-portrait *American Gothic* at the Art Institute of Chicago. It's utterly of the American Midwest, and strong for that reason, but it speaks beyond any border, to a wider and responsive world. Perhaps it's impossible to define clinically that there is 'Welsh art' as such, but what I saw was art that was made in Wales, was of Wales, was made in response to this wonder-filled land, and because of its unique stimulus.

Creating the television series and exhibition changed the way I think about what is happening to the arts in Wales. It's an exciting time, with more art and more artists working here than ever before in the history of our nation. Artists from elsewhere have come to Wales in numbers never seen before. Artists from Wales are being shown in England, across the Channel and the Atlantic, to discerning and intrigued audiences. I saw a lot of new art, and met a lot of artists, but even so I know that I saw only a very small part of what is going on.

Much of the art being made here is redolent of this special place, but not constrained by it. And like much wonderful art, it is often universal in what it says and how it says it. As Martin Barlow, Director of Oriel Mostyn, said 'There are Welsh artists whose work is in some way specifically informed by their particular Welsh background, yet successfully use an artistic language which is international in its scope, that could be exhibited anywhere in the world and hold its own'.

The Land

It's obvious that the landscape was one of the first things that inspired the artists who worked here – they were surrounded by some of the most varied, dramatic and sylvan countryside on earth. And it's an ancient landscape, ancient in terms of its interaction with humankind – some of the most wonderful Neolithic and Celtic remains have been found in Wales. It's a countryside that supplied tremendous contrasts, from the crags and cwms of Snowdonia to the gentle rolling gardens of Carmarthenshire, or the blasted headlands of the Pembrokeshire coastline. What artists make of it is as varied as the land itself, and this continues to the present day. Richard Wilson's vision of *Dolbadarn Castle* ⌊ I ⌉ is quite different from Catrin Webster's contemporary distillations of the countryside viewed from bus and train windows. Yet they are the same – a struggle to try to understand, interpret and present not only what the land looks like, but how simultaneously light, air, atmosphere, and people affect it.

Richard Wilson (1713-82) born in Penegoes, Montgomeryshire was among the first great classical landscape painters here in Wales. Though of this place, he could not remain here if the early artistic talent he had exhibited was to grow. There were no academies of art in 18th century Wales (the first two small art schools were founded in 1853) so at the age of 16 Wilson went to London to be trained as a painter. Like many of the fashionable young painters of his time, he went to study with the Italian masters, firstly in Venice and then in Rome. His initial interest in becoming a portraitist faded - perhaps he was truly a Welsh country boy at heart – and landscape commanded his attention. He painted in the Alban Hills, at the Italian lakes, in Naples and at Vesuvius. But he came back – some Welsh artists, like Thomas Brigstocke (1809-81), Thomas Jones (1742-1803), Penry Williams (1800-85) or the Conwy-born artist John Gibson (1790-1866) made a successful career in Italy. Wilson's famous *Snowdon from Llyn Nantlle* [fig.1], is an ambitious painting, a perfect view of the most

[Figure 1] Richard Wilson (1713-1782)
Snowdon from Llyn Nantlle, about.1765-6
Oil on canvas, 101 × 127 cm
Board of Trustees of the National Museums & Galleries on Merseyside,
Walker Art Gallery.

perfect Welsh mountain. It was an extraordinary moment when the BBC film crew went to a lakeside field at Y Fridd Farm and set the camera on a tripod, in exactly the place where Wilson had placed his easel. Equally astonishing, the view across Llyn Nantlle to Snowdon was unchanged despite the intervening years.

Both Wilson and J.M.W. Turner (1775-1851) painted one of the most dramatically-sited castles in Wales, Dolbadarn. Both works are in the exhibition. Turner's powerful *Dolbadarn Castle* ⌊ **2** ⌉ is a wonderfully romantic view of this great Welsh castle, perched on a rock commanding Llyn Peris and Llyn Padarn. The artist not only depicted his response to the place, but was well enough informed on Welsh history to write about the 20-year imprisonment there of Owain Goch, brother of Llywelyn ap Gruffydd, in the Royal Academy catalogue:

How awful is the silence of the waste
Where Nature lifts her mountains to the sky
Majestic solitude, behold the Tower
Where Hopeless Owen, long imprisoned, pined
And wrung his hands for liberty, in vain

Wilson's painting ⌊ **1** ⌉ of the early 1760s is a testimony to the lessons he'd learned in Italy about pictorial composition and handling of paint. It's in a well-defined tradition called the Picturesque – a style that shows a feeling for the antique, classical buildings and ruins, elegiac mood and qualities of light, contrasts between calm and high drama. Such paintings are carefully constructed – Catrin Webster observed how composed, orchestrated and 'how like a stage set' they are. But Wilson was able to convey more than the component parts of Picturesque art, he could convey respect for the landscape, and a personal experience of the moods of Nature.

Wilson's genius is in part in his ability to make a magnificent synthesis, joining an absolutely Welsh subject with the soft light and gentle air of the Roman *campagna*. It ennobled his Welsh subjects, linking them with a lofty European tradition, and introduced British grand-manner painters like Turner to the glories of the Welsh landscape. He was greatly respected by his contemporaries, even Sir Joshua Reynolds wrote of his regard for Wilson. His influence on that father-figure of British landscape, the great John Constable, was profound – Constable wrote: 'I recollect nothing so much as a solemn – bright – warm – fresh - landscape by Wilson, which still swims in my brain like a delicious dream'.

By the 1760s the wildness of nature in Wales attracted many artists, but as the landscape came under increasing cultivation the contrasts between the sublime and beautiful scenery and the untouched rugged north became even more inspirational. The English painter Thomas Rowlandson's droll self-portrait (1794) as an *Artist Travelling in Wales* [fig.2] shows that he was a seasoned visitor, struggling through the countryside on a pack-horse loaded with everything from his easel to his kettle – and with a spectacularly runny nose. During the Napoleonic Wars, Wales was the understudy for the Continental mountains and landscapes, made inaccessible by the conflict, so Snowdonia and rugged north Wales provided a domestic substitute for the Alps. Wales became a gigantic open-air studio, and it has remained so.

Today the landscape artist is looking for something different from the perfect view of unblemished Nature. David Nash (born 1945) is an internationally known artist, a sculptor who should be described as a 'land-artist' rather than a 'landscape-artist'. He doesn't make portraits of the land, rather he works in partnership with the landscape. He has created major works from Chicago to Kyoto, but his home base is a converted chapel in Blaenau Ffestiniog. Much of his work is in wood, most of it locally found, but the wood means much more than just the material from

[Figure 2] Thomas Rowlandson (1756-1827)
.An Artist travelling in Wales, 1799
Aquatint on paper, 33.5 x 39 cm
National Museums & Galleries of Wales NMW A 13683

[Figure 3] David Nash (b.1945)
The Fletched-over Ash Dome

which to sculpt shapes. The complex organic quality of the trees from which the wood is harvested provides David with inspiration. What happened to it in the process of growth, how can he work with its characteristics, 'partner' with the material to make the final work? We exhibited *Scribed Wall Leaner* of 1999 ⌊ **10** ⌉, made in redwood.

Much of David Nash's work is a collusion with Nature, and cannot be exhibited in museums or galleries. It belongs to the land where it was made, and includes permanent living sculptures growing and changing, tended over the decades by the artist. Much of David's work is private and secreted away, hidden from view. You'd be lucky indeed to stumble upon a complex work using growing trees in a hidden Welsh glade. A ring of ash plantings, placed in 1977, has been carefully guided to create a magical living tent-like canopy, *The Fletched-over Ash Dome* [fig.3], in a remote Welsh forest, growing slowly in the very landscape that inspired him. Many artists have taken from the landscape, David is that rare artist who gives Art back to Nature.

Nash's work is often about process, and the sculpture is a product that evolves from that process. Sometimes the process itself entails the actual loss or destruction of the sculptural object. The work becomes an idea in motion. For over 20 years David has been watching the process and progress of a large boulder-like orb of wood, carved from a 200-year old fallen tree - he created a dynamic mobile relationship between his wooden boulder and its surroundings, by placing it in a nearby stream. He has watched and recorded the slow progress of the boulder as the stream carried it down the mountainside. It's been beaten and battered in floods, tumbled over rocks and waterfalls, dried and split in a drought; and its form has changed. Now, it's just a few metres from entering a powerful river. When it does, it's unlikely that David Nash will see it again. The documentation of its epic journey will remain, and is as much the artwork as the boulder itself. David's happy to see it close to escape after 20 years in the little stream: "It was from this parish, from this county, from this country, now it goes into the river that goes to the sea, and it goes into the world". Its story continues, but he can no longer tell it.

Over the centuries the Welsh landscape has been a magnet for an extraordinary range of artists. Turner and Wilson are the great names, but there are plenty of others, like Graham Sutherland (1903-80) and John Piper (1903-92), both of whom came here many times to work directly from the Welsh landscape. Sutherland is best known here for his fascination with the wind-bent hedgerows of west Wales, drawn full of twisted and angry roots and thorns, with the menace of the darkest Surrealism. We chose a rather different subject from the often-seen Pembrokeshire works, *Public House & Masonic Hall in Wales* ⌊ **5** ⌉ a view of the Swansea Blitz. John Piper was connected with Wales through his wife, the writer Myfanwy Evans, and his paintings are topographical records as well as evocations of the atmosphere. We've chosen this fine watercolour of the great lost country house *Hafod* ⌊ **4** ⌉ as representative of Piper's ability to capture both. For Augustus John (1878-1961), and his painting partner James Dickson Innes (1887-1914), for whom the area around Mount Arenig ⌊ **3** ⌉ became an obsession, wild Wales was a sort-of Celtic Tahiti, as meaningful as the South Seas had been to Gauguin. Innes painted this landscape in colours of extraordinary intensity, reflecting not only his own originality, but a familiarity with new ideas on painting in Europe and the wider world.

An artist who in a large sense extends the classic approach to the landscape, recording with undimmed passion the land, its people and its seasons, is Sir Kyffin Williams (born 1918). Through sun, snow and storm, Kyffin has celebrated the vagaries of rural life in, especially, North Wales, for over half a century. The rich thickly-impasto'd works are instantly recognisable, they have become icons, a way of seeing the Welsh landscape that communicates its moods in a forceful and gripping style. They are storms on canvas, reflecting the enduring drama and power of this landscape. If one thinks of *Salem* as the

most utterly sentimental view of old Wales, these works are the opposite, unsentimental, unflattering, robust, gutsy ⌊ **7** ⌉. They are made of paint, but built like sculpture, great thick slabs of colour, tone and line that carry the story. He had a remarkable and productive visit to the Welsh community in Chubut, Patagonia, in faraway Argentina, but most of his mature landscape work and his portraits have all been made in Wales. In his voluminous writing and in interviews he has been a passionate advocate of the essence of Welshness contained in the landscape - a seam of endless inspiration for an artist who loves this land, and finds everything he ever wanted all around him.

Kyffin Williams is an elder statesman of art in Wales, as is Arthur Giardelli (born 1911), and while the character of the work is quite different, they share a fascination with the landscape. Arthur works in a 20th century idiom, utilising collage and found objects. His role in Welsh art goes beyond what he creates in the studio, for as one of the founders of the 56 Group Wales, he too has long been an ambassador and advocate of Welsh art. He's not Welsh, but Wales is in his blood, and has been since he was evacuated to Dowlais from the London Blitz in World War II. In his Pembrokeshire home/gallery/studio, its walls shaking from the vibrations of passing armoured vehicles and explosions on the Army's Castlemartin Tank Range, he works with materials found on the nearby beaches, in the landscape, and collected on his travels - pieces of washed-up wood, cork, twigs, bits of clocks, and rolls of paper. His 'assemblages' or 'constructions' transform these base materials into eloquent statements of the landscape and forms of Nature. He likes to quote the 18th century French painter Chardin: 'The eye needs to be taught how to look at Nature. How many have never seen and never will see her – and that is the anguish of the artist's life.' Words that apply to many artists represented in this exhibition. I asked Arthur to lend a work that is about what he calls 'the miracle, the mystery, the sacrament' of making work that refers to Nature. It's a mixed-material relief, with a title derived from Blake's *Tyger*, called *Forests of the Night* ⌊ **6** ⌉. It's an abstract composition, but it embodies a transforming and specific experience, of an Arthur so penniless that he'd sleep in his old car when out on the road teaching for the Extra-mural Department at Aberystwyth. Waking as dawn broke in a woodland full of Celtic mystery, he saw a watery golden sun break through the mist behind the trees in a forest that he says was 'all the forests that have ever been'. That experience resulted in this lovely, elegant and elegiac work.

Terry Setch's approach to the landscape is quite different from Kyffin's, but he shares a similar passion. His work is exhibited internationally, but it originates in and is specifically about the beaches of South Wales, and his fascination with the flotsam and jetsam washed up by the tide. His committed and concerned approach to landscape is about Wales as a lode of source-material, but reflects his interest in the work of the American abstract expressionist painters, rather than the distant traditions of Turner or Wilson. And for Terry, the Welsh beaches are his palette. Born in 1936, Setch studied in the 1950s, when ideas about what art could be, and what it could be about, were changing quickly. He extends the found-object tradition in 20th century art by employing the shoreline detritus found near his home and studio. He alters the history and identity of the things he selects from the tidewash, transforming them into works of art sealed within his paintings ⌊ **8** ⌉.

Like Terry Setch, the North Wales painter Peter Prendergast (born 1946) is an artist who is more interested in the landscape as it has been affected by the activity of humankind than in simply depicting natural beauty. He has chosen hard subject matter, hard to work with, hard to work in, hard to get across the strength of his response, hard to compress the enormity of it onto a canvas. The artist is completely overwhelmed by a location like Penrhyn Slate Quarry, a vast hole in the ground that has a terrifying climate of its own, but Peter's wonderful direct works are an act of dedication — he said that all he wanted to do was to paint "the best and most honest picture I can make of the land that I work in every day". His sense of awe is palpable in the works he has made in that impossible place, and you can see it in *Penrhyn Quarry* ⌊ **11** ⌉.

Pictures are often acts of love, and Peter's feelings for the landscape speak clearly in his paintings. They are not the simple rendering of the scene, and they are far from the classical clarity of Wilson. Peter Prendergast's work is not only about the subjects he chooses — all near his home in Deiniolen — but about the physical act of making a painting, about drawing, colour, wash and tone, scumble, and how to make those elements sing and dance. But look beyond the animated surfaces of his paintings and you'll see an artist-doctor at work, diagnosing, looking, listening, analysing what gave the North Wales landscape its condition. He has an x-ray vision that sees the skeleton of Wales under the flesh and muscle of the hills, and what humankind has laid upon the land, the roads, fields, quarries and chapels, and the relationship between them all.

What Peter Prendergast seeks to achieve is a distillation. It's more about essence than a photographic reality. It's also about the present literally laid on top of the past in the physical act of making the painting. Geoffrey Olsen ⌊ **9** ⌉ works in this way, joining themes from the Merthyr landscape to those of Italy — he's a contemporary Welsh artist who followed in Wilson's footsteps to paint in Rome. Back home in the Cotswold hills, he makes works which layer image and history, text, references to medieval frescoes, autobiographical notes, quotes from defined styles of art, combinations of abstract expressionism and meticulous realism, all overpainted many times. Each new wash is a thin veil that covers and anchors what has gone before, submerging it but not hiding it — look carefully and you'll see the deep space beyond the painting's surface.

A young artist whose work goes even further along these lines is Catrin Webster, whose paintings are about what it feels like to be in the Welsh landscape, or travelling through it, not what it actually looks like. She's asking us as viewers to define landscape, while she's redefining it herself, asking what that word is supposed to mean today. In the mid '90s she made a series of works that you could call 'landscapes', though none were conventional scenic views – and this in part is due to the way she made them. Catrin presents visual experiences taken from journeys through Wales in cars, buses and trains, viewing the landscape in motion through the window-frames of those vehicles. From the blurry snap-shots of the hardly-seen and quickly-glimpsed, she cleverly crystallizes images of many towns and villages, and many landscapes, and the journeys that connect them. The 'view' is still central to the way we see and understand the landscape, but contemporary artists have shown that views can be presented in very different ways – whether you hike up Snowdon, or see the fleeting landscape through the steamy window of a bus. It's a new way of looking at the same old Wales.

Memory and Imagination

[Figure 4] John Meirion Morris (b.1936)
Modron, 1994
Bronze, 70 x 37.5 x 23 cm
Collection of the Artist.

Stories, both real and imagined, have played a vital part in Welsh life - with myth, verifiable history and legend, they are the matter that bind Wales together, and they have provided artists with a wealth of material from which to create. Thomas Jones's famous picture *The Bard* ⌊ **12** ⌉ of 1774 is based on the legendary tale of Edward I's massacre of the Welsh bards. In it you see the last surviving member of his breed cursing the English invaders before throwing himself to his death in the river below. Dead fellow bards litter the middle distance, and a fantasy based on Stonehenge dominates the background. Did it happen, and if so, did it look like this? And does it matter ? It's a great story for a painting, and a more melodramatic tableau one couldn't imagine. Thomas Jones (1742-1803) was a painter who took directly from the deep wells of Welsh storytelling, while Sir William Goscombe John's (1860-1952) three-dimensional double-portrait in bronze brings to life *Merlin and Arthur* ⌊ **14** ⌉. This kind of narrative art was once hugely popular, and contemporary painters have not abandoned this tradition. Instead, they have found new ways to ponder the great literary traditions, and to present them without resort to descriptive illustration.

As we filmed *Memory and Imagination*, we went to an atmospheric churchyard at Nevern in Pembrokeshire, which holds a number of important clues to the richness of the

[Figure 5]
Celtic ornament on a plaque from a metalworker's horde found at Tal-y-Llyn,
Merioneth, probably 1st century AD
National Museums & Galleries of Wales

Welsh imagination. It contains a thousand-year old Celtic Cross, one of the most perfect examples of its kind. But what do all those signs and symbols scribed onto the cross really mean? Ribbons with no beginning or end have been interpreted as symbols of eternity, but it is precisely this fluidity of interpretation that makes ancient Celtic artifacts such a rich source of imaginative material for contemporary artists. In the work of the sculptor John Meirion Morris (born 1936) you have an artist trained in a Classical tradition, whose new work is informed by a living Celtic tradition. These works [fig.4] amalgamate his personal vision with those traditions, in what he calls 'images of the mind'. In the National Museum & Gallery is a small but extraordinarily beautiful metal relief sculpture called the Tal-y-Llyn shield [fig.5], made some 2000 years ago. Look at it and see the thread of Celtic continuity that links the work of the ancient past to that of a fine contemporary sculptor.

As is so often the case in Wales, stories attach themselves to anything that hangs around for long enough. We filmed at Nevern because it's a place and a landscape notable for an exceptionally rich history. It's loaded with stories. It's said that the cuckoo first arrives in Wales on the 7 April each year - and it sings its first song of the season perched on the top of that Celtic cross at Nevern. Apparently, the vicar of the church used to delay Mass on that day until the cuckoo's song was heard. One year, the bird was very late arriving and the congregation waited patiently. Eventually the cuckoo arrived - but it was so exhausted that after singing for a brief moment it died. Such storytelling is organic, it is polished and honed and, most importantly, told or pictured from multiple vantage points. Anecdotes like that at Nevern fed the imagination of the creators of some of the most extraordinary stories ever written. And to link to them, also in this glorious churchyard, is the memorial to the Rev. John Jones, Poet, Scholar, Patriot, and Vicar of this parish - but perhaps most significantly, the man who worked with Lady Charlotte Guest in translating *The Mabinogi* into English. We were able to look at

manuscripts of these legendary tales at the National Library of Wales, Aberystwyth. Of all the myths, stories and legends of Wales (so loved by David Jones) that have nourished the artist's imagination over the last century, it is the fantastic tales of *The Mabinogi* that take pride of place in a state of literary and cultural perfection. They are mysterious and complex, telling of battles, courts, romances and rivalries, maidens and monsters. They comprise the folk-memory of Wales, full of Celtic myth and magic. They were not translated and published in English until the 19th century. These were tales from the oral tradition; they trained the memory and were to be spoken to a audience, but it was in book form that they became widely accessible.
However ancient and strange these stories seem, they still somehow connect with the here and now - and it's these stories that have provided artist Ivor Davies (born 1935) with much of his raw material in recent years. And not just the *Mabinogi,* for Ivor's work also draws on Arthurian legends, early Celtic Christian myths and history – and especially on the 'idea of Wales' going back 3000 years. Mythic figures and forces like Taranedd, the god of thunder, make an appearance in his work. An atmospheric painting ⌊ **17** ⌉ in this exhibition extrapolates the story of the Santelios (St. Teilo), and the miracle of the holy book he was reading when overtaken by a terrible storm, but which remained dry throughout the downpour. He's in the picture of course, but so are coded references to Welsh history of the 19th and 20th centuries that the viewer has to explore and connect up across the decades – you'll find among them Welsh Blacks, burned cottages, the skulls of mountain ponies, a portrait of William Williams Pantycelyn, and abandoned cars. Ivor is a passionate painter, with a passion for telling and showing the turbulent ancient and contemporary histories of Wales. His paintings are a slice through that history, like geological strata, showing story and image and history piled and compressed one on top of the other.

But Ivor is also a wonderful painter, not just a spell-binding storyteller, who knows how to make the surface of the work come to life. The physical form of this painting is equally deeply of Wales – it's painted using a vibrant red earth dug up by the artist near Upper Chapel, and mixed with oil gesso to create a painting medium. In this way the artist has quite literally joined a story from the ancient 'matter' of Welsh mythology with the actual 'matter' of the very earth that supported and nourished those stories. It's disarmingly simple, but lyrical, lovely, and moving.

Iwan Bala (born 1956) has become an important voice in Wales, an artist speaking for other artists as an advocate and an organizer. But he's also as a critic and thought-provoking observer who has written at length on the current 'state of the art' and on issues of national identity, as well as looking at what he describes as 'a culture of rupture and reinvention'. It's for that reason that we asked Iwan specifically for the loan of *Pair* ⌊ **19** ⌉, which is rooted in the stories of the *Mabinogi,* but has a resonate reference to the culture and politics of Wales in the 21st century. In the legend of Bendigeidfran and Bronwen, there appears the cauldron of rebirth – dead warriors were immersed in its magical boiling water, and returned to life, but without the power of speech. Iwan Bala asks us to think about this in respect to the fight to sustain the Welsh language – it's a warning that even a renaissance of Welsh culture could be at the expense of our mother tongue. He uses an ancient mythology to capture a psychological truth that is part of contemporary Wales.

It's not just stories that have caught the artists' imagination, but story-tellers as well. It's no surprise that the ruddy face of the young Dylan Thomas ⌊ **36** ⌉ appealed to the flamboyant Augustus John; what is more intriguing is that Dylan Thomas's complex poetry became the key inspiration on one of the most significant Welsh artists of the 20th century, Ceri Richards (1903-71). The National Museum & Gallery has a wonderful painting by Ceri Richards, an explosion of animal and vegetable forms called the *Cycle of Nature* [fig.6] - one of several works inspired by the energy of the natural world, and by that mysterious poem of Thomas's called *The Force that Through The Green Fuse Drives*

[Figure 6]
Ceri Richards (1903-1971)
Cycle of Nature, 1944
Oil on canvas, 102.2 x 152.7cm
National Museums & Galleries of Wales NMW A 219

the Flower. Go and see it - it joins two of the most lyric and fertile of imaginations. But it also shows one of the reasons why Ceri Richards left Wales for London – at that time he couldn't see here enough work by his British or Continental contemporaries. The painting demonstrates his complete understanding of Surrealism and how fully he had absorbed the work of Picasso, without for a moment diluting the originality of his ideas and his expression of them.

For this exhibition we've obtained a rarely-seen and spectacular painting from a private collection, *Black Apple of the Gower* ⌊ **16** ⌉, of 1952, which the artist dedicated to Dylan Thomas. No such fruit appears in the Celtic legends, or in a history of the Gower, but it sounds as though it might have. What the artist actually did was to invent a new mythic form, paraphrased from his deep study of Celtic legends and from his drawings inspired by Dylan Thomas's poem. These were actually drawn in the volumes themselves, into the margins and the blank pages, intimately linked to Dylan's words. In demonstrating that link, the critic Mel

Gooding revealed a letter in which Ceri Richards wrote of this painting: 'It expresses for me the great richness, the fruitfulness and great cyclical movement and rhythms of the poems of Dylan. The circular image… is the metaphor expressing the sombre germinating force of Nature – surrounded by the petals of a flower, and seated within the earth and sea'.

Life is full of odd and often unexplained events. What stories do is try and account for the oddness of life. At Nevern is a strange tree known as the Bleeding Yew because it excretes a kind of reddish plasma - an odd and inexplicable characteristic, unheard of in the world of yew trees. It is of course accompanied by a story – another of those 'Strange Tales from Wales' - of a monk hanged for stealing the church's silver plate. Before putting his head in the noose, the monk cried out that the yew would bleed forever as testimony to his innocence. It's a nice story, and of course I believe every word, as many artists would, and see it as the jumping-off point for a painting.

From Hell To Heaven

One of the great themes of art in Wales in the past 200 years has been about what lies beneath the landscape. Under the beautiful coverlet of verdant Wales was buried treasure – vast seams of coal, metals and slate. Miners and quarry-men ripped aside that coverlet to get their hands on that treasure, and Wales was transformed.

The arrival of the Industrial Revolution was spectacular, and no-one had ever seen such sights. The massive excavations which formed the slate quarries of North Wales, the heat and terror of the iron-smelting blast-furnaces in the southern valleys, the deep dangerous shafts of the coal-mines, were an 'industrial picturesque', fear-inducing, and dramatic subjects for artists. The owners wanted a record of the glory of industry. Artists came from far beyond Wales to depict its processes. Some of them turned from depicting the beauty of the glorious land to celebrating the heroic grandeur of its destroyers. That's not to say that they weren't good artists, they were. Not only that, they were brilliant topographers, giving us a carefully-composed record of everything from copper mining at Mynydd Parys, slate quarrying at Bethesda, and the building of the Menai and Britannia bridges, to iron-puddlers at Rhymni. They are amazing paintings, and a grand record of their time, depicting a kind of industrial-process-as-theatre. *Cyfarthfa Ironworks* ⌊ **22** ⌉ by Penry Williams (1802-85), and *An Iron Forge at Merthyr Tydfil* ⌊ **20** ⌉ by the splendidly-named Julius Caesar Ibbotson (1759-1817), are two excellent examples – and there are hundreds more.

But I'm more interested in the art that came from the society that industry created, the culture of the mining valleys, the sense of tight-knit communities, conditioned by the invasive influence of the Nonconformist denominations. Life swung between the grind of industrialisation and the pulpit-promise of eternal reward.

The miners led a vertical life; below were pits full of coal and ore, places of danger, toil and pain, above was Paradise, and in-between, a sort of halfway house for the faithful, was the Chapel. The overwhelming power of the Chapel, and to a lesser extent the Anglican Church, developed in virtual lock-step with the explosion of the industrial revolution in Wales. The close relationship between expanding industry and the religious revivals has been widely studied, and the ubiquity of the Nonconformist belief-structure was extraordinary – industry drove the economy, but Chapel drove everything else. Chapels were places of worship, but also schools, libraries, museums of local history and the only places where works of art could be seen. The industrial owners and managers wanted chapel-men in their works, men who were sober, industrious, thrifty. In coal-and-steel boom-towns with rocketing populations like Merthyr and Dowlais, 65% of the population attended a chapel, while in the neighbouring Monmouthshire there were enough chapels to seat 75% of the county's inhabitants.

So it's not surprising that art, industry and chapel all came together in one picture. The picture. The icon, the Mona Lisa of Wales … *Salem* ⌊ **23** ⌉ by the Devon painter Curnow Vosper (1866-1942). It is the quintessential image by which Wales is known, and which still seems to represent old Wales in the public consciousness. By the time Vosper painted it in 1908, the great religious revivals were over, and this striking image of a chapel-driven life, with the matriarchal figure in traditional Welsh dress, was already fading away. Its popularity exploded when it was bought by Lord Leverhulme, the owner of Sunlight Soap. As a marketing incentive, reproductions of the picture were given away with cakes of Sunlight. Thus it ended up on thousands of walls in Wales. Although the original doesn't live here, it's at the Lady Lever Art Gallery at Port Sunlight, near Liverpool, it's good to see it 'back home' in this exhibition. And a surprise attends it – the artist's virtually unknown second version of the same subject ⌊ **24** ⌋.

It's a painting loaded with symbolism, and still retains its potency. It's full of stories, some of them real – the chapel still exists, the shawled lady and some of the others are portraits of real people, though one is imaginary and was painted from a dressed-up dummy. From the outset, many simply could not take the work at face value, and asked what exactly it meant. Vosper expresses humble religious devotion, but the ostentatious cape worn by the central figure was a surprise. Some read stories into it – seeing the face of The Devil in the folds of the richly textured shawl – puzzling whether the old lady is entering or leaving the chapel. Is she early or late? Is she guilty of the sin of Pride by wearing such a splendid Paisley shawl in this austere little chapel? Are others in the congregation in sinful Envy, coveting that shawl? Is this nostalgia for the piety of the past, or a sharp caricature of religious hypocrisy? It's easy to see why this work had such a tremendous impact, and still does. The contemporary artist Iwan Bala has investigated and analysed it at great length, and has made new works that explore the issues raised by the original. It's a painting that provokes and fascinates - a morality play in paint.

Salem reproductions hung on many a Welsh wall in the early years of this century, but a generation or two earlier pious families had hung prints of famous preachers in their homes. These were 'posters' of the hottest 'entertainers' of the day, the evangelical fire-and-brimstone revivalists who could drive a congregation to terror or religious ecstasy. Having such an image in one's parlour was a constant reminder that the Lord's ministers were keeping an eye on you. In the case of the Rev. Christmas Evans, it was literally a single eye, because the other blind socket was sewn shut. William Roos's (1808-78) original confrontational portrait ⌊ **25** ⌋, from which the prints were made, is shown here in contrast with Vosper's gentle image of Chapel. It's not

difficult to imagine the reaction of a congregation when 'Old One Eye' skewered you with his burning glare - if this man told you Heaven or Hell awaited, and that you'd better get your spiritual life in order, you believed him. Roos's painting captures the sheer physical power of the man – who was, reputedly, seven feet tall.

If the Welsh working man's home was simply furnished, with perhaps an occasional reproduction, such as Salem, then the workplace itself was, for most, a grimly dangerous place. For a long time, the only depictions of working life were created by artists from 'outside'. There were very few artists from within that working culture to give us a true picture of what it was really like – though Vincent Evans's (1895-1976) mining pictures [fig.7] from the 1930s are brilliant (as is his huge paean of praise *A Welsh Family Idyll*). When the work of Nicholas Evans (born 1907), the artist-miner, was first exhibited in London in the 1970s his directness and powerful drawing invited parallels with an artist whose early work was also chronicled the life of the working class. Nicholas Evans was hailed as 'the van Gogh of the Valleys.'

The world that Nicholas Evans painted has all but disappeared. The collieries have almost all gone, though the terraced streets of the Rhondda still snake along the steep hillsides. Artists made works that were gritty and realistic, landscapes not bathed in an impressionist glow, but often painted in soot and rain, with the pall of pollution creating a grainy haze over everything. At first this seems to be unlikely subject matter, but look how powerfully it's been expressed. The shapes and forms of this familiar industrial landscape have provided artists like George Chapman (1908-1993), Charles Burton (born 1929) and Jack Jones (1922-1993) with the subject of much of their work. An earlier generation is represented by a brooding but luminous painting by Cedric Morris (1889-1982), *The Tips, Dowlais* ⌊ **26** ⌋. Jack Jones's intense little painting, expressed with the naivete and directness of a child's vision, boils the whole valley scene down to its fundamental elements – big black coal tips, two chapels and a pub – it's called *Horeb, Zoar, and The Villiers* ⌊ **30** ⌉.

Other artists focussed on the heroic worker, rather than the industrial landscape, and of these perhaps the most renowned is Josef Herman (1911-2000). A Polish Jew steeped in the history and practice of art in Europe, he escaped the Nazis, and ended up in the mining community of Ystradgynlais in 1944. The impact of the Welsh landscape, and the men and women who lived in it, was a riveting inspiration. He became part of the community – they all went down to Swansea to see his exhibition – but they'd thought at first he was some wealthy eccentric who had settled among them for unknowable reasons. Then, the artist recalled, 'they found out that I made less money than a trainee collier.' He stayed in that close but welcoming community for many years, only illness drove him to leave, and in Spain, Italy and Israel his work continues the theme of physical work, a legacy of the men and women of the Welsh mining valleys. His monumental

paintings are poems of praise to the dignity of labour, depicting miners as massive sculptural forms, men who could hold up the world. One evening Herman saw the colliers coming home over a long railway bridge, and it was a scene that he never forgot: 'The image of the miners on that bridge, against a glowing sky and a great golden sun, had a feeling that mystified me for years, a mixture of sadness and grandeur, and it became the source of my work for the rest of my life.'

In his studio hung the archetypal Herman, his favourite portrait subject 'Mike the Miner'. He also painted groups that were heroic in both subject and style. His magnificent mural commissioned for the 1951 Festival of Britain is awesome and humbling – and too large for this exhibition. We show here *Miners Singing* ⌊ **29** ⌉, a study for it. Did you know that the average amount of time a museum visitor spends in front of a work of art is just 9. 5 seconds? (It's true, there's an extensive American study on this). Well, Herman's mural made me stop dead in my tracks,

[Figure 7] Vincent Evans (1895-1976)
Repairing Main Road, 1936
Oil, 100.5 x 125.5 cm
National Museums & Galleries of Wales NMWA 15020

[Figure 8]
David Garner (b.1958)
Aberfan
School chairs, bitumen and coal, childs blackboard, size variable.
The Artist

and I didn't move for a very long time. Go and see it at the Glynn Vivian Gallery in Swansea, you'll see what I mean. Herman was a seminal figure in what happened to art in Wales, particularly in resolving the role of the figure within the fabric of painting. But he was not alone in his intense study of the working figure – Will Roberts' farmers have equally grand power, as does the work of many other artists we could not include. A fine example is *Hedger and Ditcher, a Portrait of William Lloyd* ⌊ **28** ⌉, by an introspective artist who worked in virtual isolation in Flint, Albert Houthuesen (1903-79), who was born in Holland, studied in London, and then settled in Wales.

Most of the artists I've referred to are painters, and all have worked directly from industrial inspiration, or the culture of the mining valleys and the farming communities. Painters like Jack Crabtree (born 1938) and Ernie Zobole (1927-99) (and I was lucky enough to be taught by both of them, and by John Selway, at Newport) have continued to present very differing ways of telling the story of the

process and the effects of industrialisation, what it looked like and what it meant, and its effect on the lives of the communities formed by it. But that landscape is not the exclusive domain of painters. Tony Stevens (born 1928) was Head of Fine Art and of Sculpture at Newport College of Art, and was highly influential as an artist, teacher and mentor. His wonderful large mixed-media sculpture *Rainy Day in Wales* ⌊ **31** ⌉ captures all the forms one would see on a depressing wet Wednesday in Williamstown. The shiny slates on a stylized terrace of houses are made of polished aluminium, the sooty crows are in black fibreglass, as is the gloomy cloud spitting metal rods of rain. A friend said this work was 'so absolutely real that it's actually abstract.'

Wales was the first nation to industrialise, and the first to enter the post-industrial world. South Wales was the crucible of innovation and invention in industry, but heavy industry is now largely a thing of the past. But what interests me is that there is a whole generation of artists who seem haunted by the memories of our industrial history. They seem compelled to reinvigorate our thinking about the present through a series of reflections on our past. The Welsh valleys were extraordinary places in which to be brought up and to live, and sociologists have commented on these communities at length. And they were real communities, places where people relied on each other, and there was a sense of caring spirit. Chapel had released its traditional hold on the population, socialism was the political bedrock, and a sense of common decency informed one's day-to-day life. There was a political dialogue that was stuffed with idealism and hope, and radicals spoke with a passionate eloquence informed by that earlier generation, those 'kings of the pulpit', the chapel preachers. Evan Walters' (1893-1951) theatrical painting *The Communist* ⌊ **27** ⌉ acts here as a representative of those ideals in action. People would pull together when things went wrong, and in industrial Wales they sometimes went wrong in a very big way. The horror of the Aberfan disaster inspired David Garner's installation work [fig.8] which, because of its scale, we could not

show, but it is an impressive and disturbing achievement. It's a hard look at a subject that's hard to look at, and a tragedy almost too difficult to contemplate.

The art of industry that once flourished in Wales has swung full circle. It began with outsiders capturing images of a kind of living hell on earth. They had a sense of 'This is a great visual drama, but thank God I don't have to live here.' In the mid-20th century artists reappraised their surroundings, making a passionate and committed art, from understanding the inside of the Welsh workers' culture. Now artists look back to the beginning, knowing all that has happened since within a culture still coming to terms with that past, and facing an uncertain future. Tragedy and heroism are constant themes in the art that emerged from the rise and fall of industry in Wales. For 200 years it's provided rich source material for artists. So I have to wonder about what kind of art, if any, will be made in the future that is about the 'history of industry', for the real thing will soon be only a memory.

The Figure

As elsewhere, the figure has been an important subject for artists in Wales, but perhaps more than anywhere else, the depiction of the human form seems to have split into two. On the one hand, there has been a fascination with rural and industrial life, with the figure in or under the land – farmers on the surface and miners beneath it. On the other, there is a strong tradition of classical portraiture, where the figure or face is central to the composition and is therefore usually abstracted from its surroundings. This, I suppose is more of a metropolitan response to the human form – and it was for long comparatively rare. Things seem to have changed after the 1920s, perhaps as the grip of Nonconformity relaxed, for Chapel did not encourage pictorial investigations of 'sensuality' or the painting the unadorned figure for the 'pleasure of relishing its innate beauty'.

Some might also say that the rigidity of Calvinist thinking was 'to blame' for the slower development of the visual arts, for the power of the Chapel was very considerable in Wales, affecting virtually every aspect of life in the community. My fellow chapel-watcher, Professor John Harvey, at Aberystwyth, has published extensively on the attitude of the 19th century Nonconformist denominations towards visual artists, and the role of the human figure in their art. Mostly the artist was an illustrator, bringing to life the Bible stories, and providing a visual aid to the preacher's Scriptural interpretations. While the denominations promoted the visual arts as an integral part of their mission, they would have had little time for art that was not directly relevant to that mission.

Nevertheless, the autonomous figure has a considerable history in painting in Wales – the portraits commissioned by the gentry being the obvious example. This exhibition includes two such portraits – one of them is the oldest work in it, the striking *Vaughan of Tretower* ⌊ **32** ⌉, painted around 1560 by an anonymous artist. The other, by Frances Cotes (1726-1770), is of *Richard Myddleton of Chirk* ⌊ **33** ⌉. The WJ Chapman picture of *David Davies, a Cinder Filler, Hirwaun* ⌊ **34** ⌉ dates from the1830s. It shows the man surrounded by swirls of smoke, and is quite amazing. It's one of a unique series of sixteen or so, commissioned by Francis, son of the ironmaster William Crawshay. Nothing like these lapidary portraits of actual working folk had previously existed, or was ever repeated. We show here only one, but they are all illustrated and their story told in a fine book by Peter Lord.[2]

Millions of photographs are made every day, and most of them are pictures of people. They may not be 'portraits' in the artist's sense, but they serve the purpose of recording appearance. When photography was invented it was said that portraiture and painting were dead. Well, they are not, and neither is painting the human figure. But because of photography the figure painter was relieved of the burden of merely recording a likeness – the camera could do that. The artist was free to look at the figure in a different way, probing psychological insights and making pictures that are 'about' rather than simply 'of' a person. Augustus John (1878-1961), a self-advertised *enfant terrible* from Tenby, did both – his portraits are startling in their life-capturing immediacy, painterly skill, and insight into the sitter. One of his best, freshest, and most famous works is shown here, the portrait of a young, alert, bright-eyed cherubic *Dylan Thomas* ⌊ **36** ⌉.

Augustus's sister, Gwen John (1876-1939), was unquestionably one of Wales's finest artists, a painter who commanded a kind of understated intensity that was a reflection of her quiet life. She'd moved to study in France, and remained there, painting personal and intimate works that seem to reach into the core of her austere

world – the opposite of the flamboyant socialising of her notorious brother. She too painted portraits, and the exhibition includes what I think of as a psychological self-portrait, though she's not actually in it. It's a picture entitled *A Corner of the Artist's Room in Paris* ⌊ **35** ⌉. It's a painting that somehow conveys so much about her life, that sense of controlled passion, of order, quiet and absolute calm. Just as many artists in Wales have been inspired by our fantastic storytelling tradition, others, mostly women, have chosen to focus on their own personal stories. Shani Rhys-James (born 1953) uses her own face and history as the jumping-off point to create intense worlds of complex relationships that, like the works of Gwen John, dwell in familiar domestic spaces. She is a quite marvellous painter, making ambitious figure compositions with tremendous confidence and authority. She lives in remotest Wales, and she got there by conscious choice, because she isn't Welsh-born. Her father is Welsh, but she came here from Australia via England. But she knew this was home, and that it destined she'd work here. As an 'outsider' who came 'inside' Wales, she brings a perspective informed by outside time and travel. She wasn't a student in Wales, but we talked about those days when I felt there was little conviction about a future for artists in Wales. Many moved away. Yet here she was, thousands of miles from Australia - talking about the sense of timing and confidence she felt - talking about the commitment of Martin Tinney, the Cardiff dealer who has done so much to promote the work of artists in Wales - talking about artists who have 'come into being, just by being here' - talking about what Wales gives to artists.

She has a fine big barn-studio, filled with fine big paintings, and some tiny ones. She's exhibited just about everywhere, and she is especially known here for the paintings specific to ideas that came to her from the Mansell double-portrait, in the collection of the National Museum & Gallery. But she's often mis-identified as a self-portraitist, though her work is more about an internal portrait – her figures bear only the faintest resemblance to

[2] Peter Lord, *The Francis Crawshay Worker Portraits,* Aberystwyth, 1996

Shani herself⌊ **40** ⌉. Painters use the figure to convey ideas about the human condition in a broader sense, and this is the case with her work. And sometimes about being an artist, painting the act of painting, pictures within pictures, the shambles of the working studio, while the paintings talk to each other.

To a great extent, the world of worker-figures which Will Roberts and Josef Herman painted has now gone. For good or ill, people have largely been relieved of that intensive hard labour. But many painters still work with the figure and the land, sometimes intertwined. In this sense, the painter Kevin Sinnott (born 1947) has taken over the baton from Herman. Sinnott paints the same kind of people - but now they seem to have more time on their hands. His characters reside on the windy hill rather than down the mine. They are young, and if not actually in love – they are certainly thinking about it. I saw an amazing work by Kevin at the Flowers East Gallery in London, some years ago. It was a valleys townscape with two running figures, and it did all the things that you're taught not to do in making a composition – like dividing it right down the middle, having big forms leading the eye out of the picture and the like. But he'd got it dead right, with such control and balance, and the calorific paint surface was like cake-icing – you wanted to lick it off. It's become quite a well-known work now, in the collection of the National Museum & Gallery, called *Running Away with the Hairdresser* [fig.9]. I thought it a cracking picture.

Kevin works in a converted church, a big studio with plenty of room to push ideas around – an arena where an artist is 'locked in unarmed combat with a canvas.' The way he worked was a surprise, considering the complex multi-figure compositions set in strongly-modelled backgrounds that he paints. I've always been fascinated by the 'engineering' of a painting or sculpture, the structure that carries the ideas. He literally pushes the paint around loosely on a bare canvas with no preparation or under-drawing. Out of the mist and mess of drips and dash

[Figure 9]
Kevin Sinnott (b.1947)
Running Away with the Hairdresser, 1995
Oil on canvas, 63 x 85 cm
National Museums & Galleries of Wales NMW A 3993

there start to appear some figure-like forms. They begin to tell him a story. A dialogue develops. It becomes a painting.

Standing in his studio I saw this happen, but it still surprised me – I have a friend in the States who creates big complicated figure subjects with lots of *sturm-und-drang* in the paint that looks very spontaneous, but her planning is meticulous. Kevin works at first like an abstract expressionist, but out of the canvas might come the football pitch, the spectators, the terraced houses, the threatening mountains, Kevin's dog, and the young lovers watching it all on the Blaengarw hillside. He studies the landscape, the people, the light, making drawings for reference and information, but not necessarily to define the composition. The act of 'starting the paint' is more fluid. He's not a landscape painter, but landscape supports the stories of those who people his work. Very occasionally, it's the artist himself. He worked in London before deciding to return to Wales, the motor that now drives his work. He came back in 1993, the wettest year on record, he said. Not the best time to go trudging around in the Llynfi Valley, but that's what he did, with sketching materials and portable easel (but no kettle or runny nose like poor old Rowlandson 200 years before). The painting that came of out those walks and the thinking that went with them is *The Artist in Retreat.* One can read it as the protagonist walking away from England, back to Wales, as though he was walking through the picture from one place to the other, on his way to the next canvas.

The artist's life is never easy, and never will be, but many of the artists I met said that, for the first time, they have felt this is beginning to be a good time to be an artist in Wales. I like to hear Catatonia and Cerys Matthews belting out 'Every day when I wake up, I thank the Lord I'm Welsh.' A lot of artists are singing the same words, as Cerys's chorus. Some are in the television programmes, or this exhibition. Other curators would choose different works in a different kind of exhibition about art in Wales. But for me, these are some of the many works that I'd love to live with every day, that would shout or whisper the part they've played in *Painting the Dragon.*

Anthony Jones,
April 2000

⌊ 1 ⌉
Richard Wilson (1713-82)
Dolbadarn Castle

⌊2⌉
J. M. W. Turner (1775-1851)
Dolbadarn Castle, about 1800

⌊ **3** ⌉
JD Innes (1887-1914)
Ranunculus, about 1912

⌊ 4 ⌉
John Piper (1903-1992)
Hafod, 1939

⌊ 5 ⌉
Graham Sutherland (1903-1992)
Public House & Masonic Hall in Wales, 1940

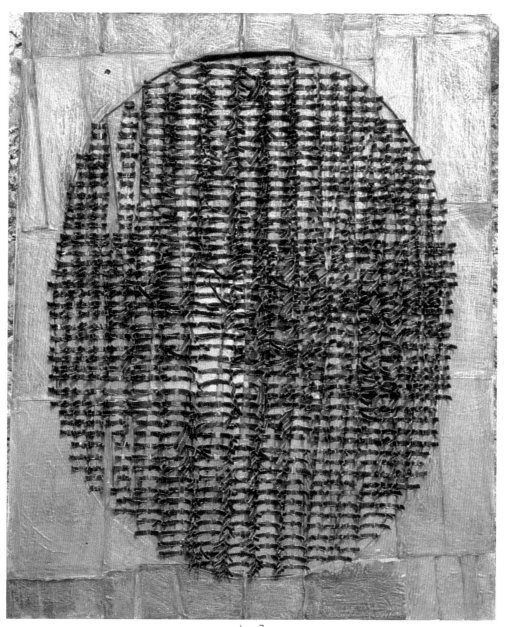

⌊6⌉
Arthur Giardelli (b.1911)
Forests of the Night 1975

⌊ 7 ⌉
Kyffin Williams (b.1918)
Penygwryd, 1998

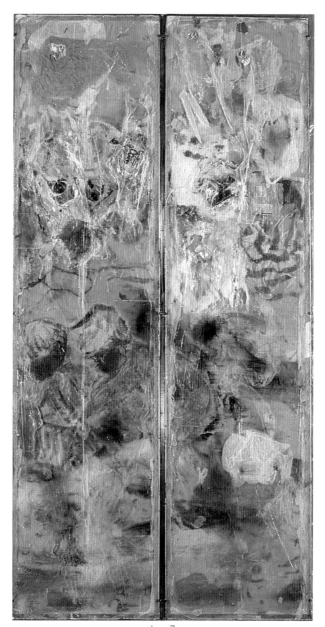

[8]
Terry Setch (b.1936)
Mudlarks, 1994/99

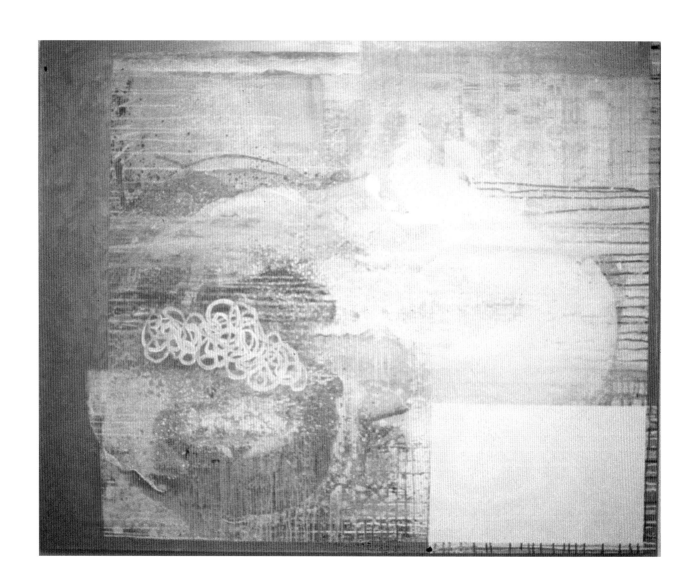

⌊ **9** ⌉
Geoffrey Olsen (b.1943)
Nurture, Extramural Series, 1998-99

[**10**]
David Nash (b.1945)
Scribed Wall Leaner, 1999

⌊ 11 ⌉
Peter Prendergast (b.1946)
Penrhyn Quarry, about 1980-81

12
Thomas Jones (1742-1803)
The Bard, 1774

⌊ **13** ⌉
Herbert von Herkomer (1849-1914)
Hwfa Môn, Arch-Druid of Wales, 1896

⌊ 14 ⌉
William Goscombe John (1860-1952)
Merlin and Arthur, about 1902

⌊ **15** ⌉
David Jones (1895-1974)
Tristan ac Essyllt, 1962

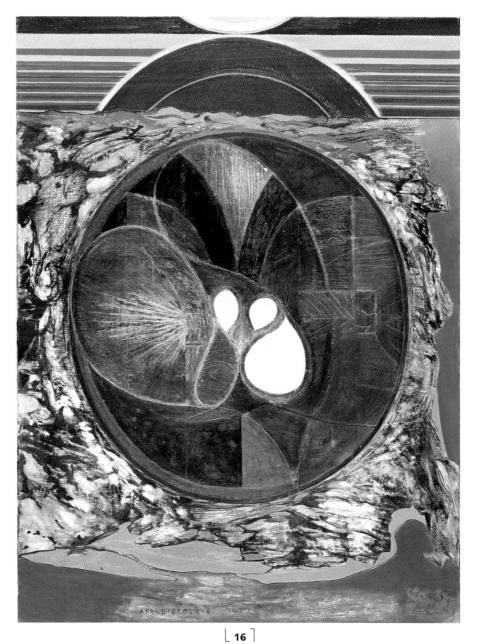

16

Ceri Richards (1903-71)
Black Apple of the Gower (Afal Du Brogwyr Gwro Gaeth I Dylan Thomas), 1952

⌊ **17** ⌉
Ivor Davies (b.1935)
Teilo, 1996

18

Clive King (b.1944)

Shelter, 1999

19
Iwan Bala (b.1956)
Pair (Dadeni ond Colli Iaith)-(Re-Birth, Lost Voice), 1997

⌊ **20** ⌉
JC Ibbetson (1759-1817)
An Iron Forge at Merthyr Tydfil, 1789

[21]
John Gibson (1790-1866)
Monument to Margaret Sandbach, about 1852

⌈ 22 ⌉
Penry Williams (1802-85)
Cyfarthfa Ironworks, about 1825

⌐ **23** ⌐
S. Curnow Vosper (1866-1942)
Salem, 1908

24

S. Curnow Vosper (1866-1942)
Salem, 1909

⌊ **25** ⌉
William Roos (1808-78)
Rev. Christmas Evans, 1832

⌐ **26** ¬
Cedric Morris (1889-1982)
The Tips, Dowlais, about 1936-9

⌐ 27 ⌐
Evan Walters (1893-1951)
The Communist, about 1932

⌊ **28** ⌉
Albert Houthuesen (1903-1979)
Hedger and Ditcher – Portrait of William Lloyd, 1937

⌊ **29** ⌉
Josef Herman (1911-2000)
Miners Singing, about 1950-51

⌐ **30** ⌐
Jack Jones (1922-93)
Horeb, Zoar and the Villiers

⌊ **31** ⌉
Tony Stevens (b.1928)
Rainy Day in Wales, 1973

32

Anon about 1560
Vaughan of Tretower

⌊ 33 ⌉
Francis Cotes (1726-70)
Richard Myddleton

[34]
WJ Chapman (active 1830s)
David Davies, Cinder Filler, Hirwaun, about 1835

⌊ **35** ⌉
Gwen John (1876-1939)
A Corner of the Artist's Room in Paris, 1907-09

[**36**]
Augustus John (1878-1961)
Dylan Thomas, 1937-38

⌐37⌐
Alfred Janes (1911-98)
Dylan Thomas, 1934

[38]
John Elwyn (1916-97)
Bore Sûl, about 1950

39
Kevin Sinnott (b.1947)
Local Passion, 1999

⌐ **40** ¬
Shani Rhys James (b.1953)
Stairs II, 1998

PAINTING THE DRAGON

Part 1: The Land

⌞1⌝ **Richard Wilson** (1713-82)
Dolbadarn Castle
Oil on canvas, 92.4 × 126.2 cm
National Museums and Galleries of Wales
NMW A 72

⌞2⌝ **J. M. W. Turner** (1775-1851)
Dolbadarn Castle, about 1800
Oil on canvas, 119.4 × 90.2 cm
Royal Academy of Arts, London

⌞3⌝ **JD Innes** (1887-1914)
Ranunculus, about 1912
Oil on panel, 24.2 × 33.2 cm
Board of Trustees of the National Museums & Galleries on
Merseyside, Walker Art Gallery

⌞4⌝ **John Piper** (1903-1992)
*Hafod,*1939
Watercolour, 38.2 × 52.8 cm
National Museums & Galleries of Wales
NMW A 1876

⌞5⌝ **Graham Sutherland** (1903-1992)
Public House & Masonic Hall in Wales, 1940
Watercolour, 53.7 × 79.6 cm
National Museums & Galleries of Wales
NMW A 3268

⌞6⌝ **Arthur Giardelli** (b.1911)
Forests of the Night about 1975
Mixed media relief, 76 × 61 × 4 cm
The Artist.

⌞7⌝ **Kyffin Williams** (b.1918)
Penygwryd, 1998
Oil on canvas, 121.9 × 121.9 cm
National Library of Wales.

⌞8⌝ **Terry Setch** (b.1936)
Mudlarks, 1994-99
Mixed media, polystyrene, 256 × 137 cm
The Artist.

⌞9⌝ **Geoffrey Olsen** (b.1943)
Nurture, Extramural Series, 1998-99
Acrylic on canvas, 120 × 150 cm
Gordon Trebilcock

⌞10⌝ **David Nash** (b.1945)
Scribed Wall Leaner, 1999
Redwood, 297 × 34 × 28 cm
Courtesy of Annely Juda Fine Art, London.

⌞11⌝ **Peter Prendergast** (b.1946)
Penrhyn Quarry, about 1980-1981
Drawing on paper, 98 × 116 cm
Lewis and Eileen Allan.

PAINTING THE DRAGON

Part 2: Memory and Imagination

⌊12⌋ **Thomas Jones** (1742-1803)
The Bard, 1774
Oil on canvas, 114.5 × 168 cm
National Museums & Galleries of Wales NMW A 85

⌊13⌋ **Herbert von Herkomer** (1849-1914)
Hwfa Môn, Arch-Druid of Wales, 1896
Watercolour,
The Forbes Magazine Collection, New York.

⌊14⌋ **William Goscombe John** (1860-1952)
Merlin and Arthur, about 1902
Bronze, 61 × 25 × 25 cm
National Museums & Galleries of Wales NMW A 127

⌊15⌋ **David Jones** (1895-1974)
Tristan ac Essyllt, about 1962
Watercolour and gouache, 77.6 × 57.4 cm
National Museums & Galleries of Wales NMWA 14926

⌊16⌋ **Ceri Richards** (1903-71)
*Black Apple of the Gower (Afal Du Brogwyr Gwro
Gaeth I Dylan Thomas)*, 1952
Oil on canvas, 100 × 75 cm
Rachel Patterson.

⌊17⌋ **Ivor Davies** (b.1935)
Teilo, 1996
Oil and oil gesso on canvas, 160 × 130 cm
The Artist.

⌊18⌋ **Clive King** (b.1944)
Shelter, 1999
Graphite on paper, 152.5 × 152.5 cm
Museum of Modern Art, Wales.

⌊19⌋ **Iwan Bala** (b.1956)
Pair (Dadeni ond Colli Iaith)-(Re-Birth, Lost Voice), 1997
Mixed media on canvas on board, 80 × 80 cm
The Artist.

PAINTING THE DRAGON

Part 3: From Hell to Heaven

⌊20⌉ **JC Ibbetson** (1759-1817)
An Iron Forge at Merthyr Tydfil, 1789
Watercolour, 22 × 29 cm
Cyfarthfa Castle Museum & Art Gallery, Merthyr Tydfil.

⌊21⌉ **John Gibson** (1790-1866)
Monument to Margaret Sandbach, about 1852
Marble
Board of Trustees of the National Museums
& Galleries on Merseyside,
Walker Art Gallery.

⌊22⌉ **Penry Williams** (1802-85)
Cyfarthfa Ironworks, about.1825
Oil on canvas, 123 × 180 cm
Private Collection.

⌊23⌉ **S. Curnow Vosper** (1866-1942)
Salem, 1908
Watercolour, 70 × 72.5 cm
Board of Trustees of the National Museums
& Galleries on Merseyside,
Lady Lever Art Gallery, Port Sunlight.

⌊24⌉ **S. Curnow Vosper** (1866-1942)
Salem, 1909
Watercolour (2nd version), 38.6 × 34.7 cm
Private Collection, on loan to National Museums & Galleries of
Wales, NMW A(L) 1160

⌊25⌉ **William Roos** (1808-78)
Rev. Christmas Evans, 1832
Oil on millboard, 39.4 × 33.2 cm
National Museums & Galleries of Wales NMW A 2410

⌊26⌉ **Cedric Morris** (1889-1982)
The Tips, Dowlais, about.1936-39
Oil on canvas, 58.5 × 71 cm
Cyfarthfa Castle Museum & Art Gallery, Merthyr Tydfil.

⌊27⌉ **Evan Walters** (1893-1951)
The Communist, about.1932
Oil on canvas, 76 × 92.1cm
National Museums & Galleries of Wales NMW A 2226

⌊28⌉ **Albert Houthuesen** (1903-1979)
Hedger and Ditcher – Portrait of William Lloyd, 1937
Oil on canvas, 234 × 101.8cm
National Museums & Galleries of Wales NMW A 11736

⌊29⌉ **Josef Herman** (1911-2000)
Miners Singing, about 1950-51
Oil on board, 43.5 × 121.6 cm
National Museums & Galleries of Wales NMW A 1674

⌊30⌉ **Jack Jones** (1922-93)
Horeb, Zoar and the Villiers
Oil on board, 42.7 × 60.5 cm
City & County of Swansea : Glynn Vivian Art Gallery

⌊31⌉ **Tony Stevens** (b.1928)
Rainy Day in Wales, 1973
Mixed media sculpture, 223 × 54 × 48 cm
The Artist.

PAINTING THE DRAGON

Part 4: The Figure

⌊32⌉ **Anon** about 1560
Vaughan of Tretower
Oil on panel, 98.4 × 72.4 cm
Edward Harley Esq.

⌊33⌉ **Francis Cotes** (1726-70)
Richard Myddleton
Oil on canvas, 127 × 101.5 cm
National Museums & Galleries of Wales NMW A 2981, on loan
to National Trust, Chirk Castle

⌊34⌉ **WJ Chapman** (active 1830s)
David Davies, Cinder Filler, Hirwaun, about 1835
Oil on canvas, 35 × 24 cm
Miss Sylvia Crawshay

⌊35⌉ **Gwen John** (1876-1939)
A Corner of the Artist's Room in Paris, 1907-09
Oil on canvas on board, 31.2 × 24.8 cm
National Museums & Galleries of Wales NMW A 3397

⌊36⌉ **Augustus John** (1878-1961)
Dylan Thomas, 1937-38
Oil on canvas, 41.4 × 35 cm
National Museums & Galleries of Wales NMW A 159

⌊37⌉ **Alfred Janes** (1911-98)
Dylan Thomas, 1934
Oil on canvas, 40.6 × 30.5 cm
National Museums & Galleries of Wales NMW A 2641

⌊38⌉ **John Elwyn** (1916-97)
Bore Sûl, about 1950
Oil on canvas, 50.5 × 61 cm
National Museums & Galleries of Wales NMW A 3917

⌊39⌉ **Kevin Sinnott** (b.1947)
Local Passion, 1999
Oil on linen, 110 × 144 cm
The Artist.

⌊40⌉ **Shani Rhys James** (b.1953)
Stairs II, 1998
Oil on canvas, 180 × 210
Courtesy of Wolverhampton Art Gallery.

PAINTING THE DRAGON

Select Bibliography

Alley, Ronald (ed.), *Graham Sutherland,* exhibition catalogue, Tate Gallery, London, 1982

Bala, Iwan (ed.), *Certain Welsh Artists : Custodial Aesthetics in Contemporary Welsh Art,* Seren, Bridgend, 1999

Bala, Iwan (ed.), *Offrymau : Ailddyferriadau / Offerings : Reinventions,* Seren, Bridgend, 2000

Bell, David, *The Artist in Wales,* George G Harrap & Co, London, 1957

Butlin, Martin, and Joll, Evelyn, *The Paintings of J. M. W. Turner,* Yale University Press, New Haven and London, 1984

Chitty, S., *Gwen John 1876-1939,* Hodder & Stoughton, London, 1981

Constable, W. G., *Richard Wilson,* Routledge & Kegan Paul, London, 1952

Curtis, Tony (ed.), *Welsh Painters Talking,* Seren, Bridgend, 1997

Ivor Davies: *Chwedloniaeth y Llyfr Gwyn / Legends from the White Book,* exhibition catalogue, Wolseley Fine Arts, London / Royal Cambrian Academy, Conwy, 1998

Evans, Mark, *Portraits by Augustus John: Family, friends and the Famous,* exhibition catalogue, National Museum of Wales, Cardiff, 1988

Evans, Mark, and Fairclough, Oliver, *A Companion Guide to the National Art Gallery,* National Museums & Galleries of Wales, Cardiff, 2nd ed. 1997

Fraser-Jenkins A. D. (ed.), *J. D. Innes at the National Museum of Wales,* exhibition catalogue, National Museum of Wales, Cardiff, 1976

Fraser-Jenkins A. D. (ed.), *John Piper,* exhibition catalogue, Tate Gallery, London, 1983

Gowing, Lawrence, *The Originality of Thomas Jones,* Thames & Hudson, London, 1985

Harvey, John, *Art of Piety : The Visual Culture of Welsh Nonconformity,* University of Wales Press, Cardiff, 1995

Harvey, John, *Image of the Invisible : The Visualisation of Religion in the Welsh Nonconformist Tradition,* University of Wales Press, Cardiff, 1999

Herman, Josef, *Related Twilights : Notes from an Artist's Diary,* Robson Books, London, 1975

Herman, Mini, *Josef Herman : A Working Life,* Quartet Books, London, 1996

Hills, P. (ed.), *David Jones,* exhibition catalogue, Tate Gallery, London, 1981

Holroyd, Michael. *Augustus John,* Chatto & Windus, London, 1996

Huntingdon-Whitely, James, *Albert Houthuesen 1903-1979: An Artist in Wales,* exhibition catalogue, Albert Houthuesen Trust, 1997

James, Merlin (ed.), *David Jones 1895-1974 : A Map of the Artist's Mind,* Lund Humphries Publishers Ltd, London, 1995

Alfred Janes 1911-1999, exhibition catalogue, Glynn Vivian Art Gallery, Swansea, 1999

Themes and Variations: The Drawings of Augustus John 1901-1931, exhibition catalogue, Lund Humphries Publishers, London, in association with the National Museums & Galleries of Wales, 1996

Bibliography

Jones, Anthony, *Welsh Chapels*, revised ed. Alan Sutton, Stroud, in association with the National Museums & Galleries of Wales, 1996

Langdale, Cecily, *Gwen John*, Yale University Press, New Haven and London, 1987

Lord, Peter, *The Francis Crawshay Worker Portraits*, National Library of Wales Aberystwyth, 1996

Lord, Peter, *The Visual Culture of Wales : Industrial Society*, University of Wales Press, Cardiff 1998

Lord, Peter, *The Visual Culture of Wales : Imagining the Nation*, University of Wales Press, Cardiff , forthcoming

Matthew, T., *The Biography of John Gibson RA, Sculptor, Rome*, William Heinemann, London 1911

Mead Johnson, Edward, *Francis Cotes*, Phaidon Press Ltd, Oxford 1976

Meyrick, Robert, *John Elwyn*, National Library of Wales, Aberystwyth 1996

Mitchell, James, *Julius Caesar Ibbetson (1759-1817)*, exhibtion catalogue, John Mitchell & Son, London, 1999

Morphet, Richard (ed.), *Cedric Morris*, exhibition catalogue, Tate Gallery, London, 1984

Ormond, John (ed.), *Kyffin Williams RA*, exhibition catalogue, National Museum of Wales, Cardiff, and Mostyn Art Gallery, Llandudno, 1987

Pearson, Fiona, *Goscombe John at the National Museum of Wales*, National Museum of Wales, Cardiff 1979

Peter Prendergast, exhibition catalogue, Oriel Mostyn Art Gallery, Llandudno, 1999

Shani Rhys James : New Paintings, exhibition catalogue, Martin Tinney Gallery, Cardiff, 1998

Rowan , Eric (ed.), *Art in Wales : An Illustrated History 2000BC-AD1850*, University of Wales Press, Cardiff 1978

Rowan, Eric, *Art in Wales : An Illustrated History 1850-1980*, University of Wales Press, Cardiff, 1985

Terry Setch, New Work. 1989-92, exhibition catalogue, Oriel Cardiff 1992

Kevin Sinnott : New Paintings, Martin Tinney Gallery, Cardiff 1999

Solkin, D. H., *Richard Wilson*, exhibition catalogue, Tate Gallery, London 1982

Wakelin, Peter, *Creu Cymuned o Arlunwyr : 50 mlynedd o'r Grwp Cymreig / Creating an Art Community : 50 Years of the Welsh Group*, National Museums & Galleries of Wales, Cardiff 1999

Webley, Derrick Pritchard, *Cast to the Winds : The Life and Work of Penry Williams (1802-1885)*, National Library of Wales, Aberystwyth, 1997

Williams, Kyffin, *The Land and the Sea*, Gomer, Llandysul, 1998

PAINTING THE DRAGON

Acknowledgements

There are far too many people to thank, all of whom made a great effort and contribution to this project, but I must especially acknowledge at BBC Wales, Dai Smith, Phil George and Richard Trayler-Smith, Steven Freer, the series producer, and Christopher Bruce, the director. Profound thanks are also due to the programme researchers, Claire Rendell and Ceri Thomas, and the heroic camera and sound-crew who braved the storms (Penrhyn Quarry in a Force 8 gale !), Catrin Mair Thomas and to Valmai Williams, who held everything together.

At the National Museum & Gallery, my debts are to Colin Ford, Director to 1998, and his successor, Anna Southall, to Oliver Fairclough, Keeper of Art, and to Mark Evans, formerly Assistant Keeper, and the art-technicians for installing the show.

My greatest thanks has to be to the artists - and their families - for they gave generously of their time and thoughts, to welcome me and the film crew into their homes and studios with good humour, endless cups of tea, and great generosity of spirit. It was an honour and a delight to have met you.

Professor Anthony Jones
The School of the Art Institute of Chicago

Photographic Acknowledgements

Works reproduced by permission of the artists, their estates and of the National Museums & Galleries of Wales.

2,	Royal Academy of Arts, London.
3, 21, 24, Fig 1,	Board of Trustees of the National Museums & Galleries of Merseyside.
5,	Prolitteris.
7,	National Library of Wales.
13,	The FORBESMagazine Collection, NewYork, © All rights reserved.
15,	Trustees of the estate of David Jones.
16, 35, Fig 6,	DACS.
20, 26,	Cyfarthfa Castle Museum, Merthyr Tydfil.
22, 32, 34,	Centre for Advanced Welsh and Celtic Studies, Aberystwyth.
28,	Albert Houthuesen Trust.
30,	City and County of Swansea, Glynn Vivian Art Gallery.